4/09

P9-DYE-031

DATE

MAY 2 6 2006

Horses

Thoroughbred
Horses

by Kim O'Brien
Consulting Editor: Gail Saunders-Smith, PhD

Capstone
press®

Mankato, Minnesota

Pebble Books are published by Capstone Press,
151 Good Counsel Drive, P.O. Box 669, Mankato, Minnesota 56002.
www.capstonepress.com

1 2 3 4 5 6 14 13 12 11 10 09

Library of Congress Cataloging-in-Publication Data
O'Brien, Kim.
    Thoroughbred horses / by Kim O'Brien.
    p. cm. — (Pebble books. Horses)
    Includes bibliographical references and index.
    Summary: "A brief introduction to the characteristics, life cycle, and uses of
the Thoroughbred horse breed" — Provided by publisher.
    ISBN-13: 978-1-4296-2236-3 (hardcover)
    ISBN-10: 1-4296-2236-9 (hardcover)
    1. Thoroughbred horse — Juvenile literature. I. Title.
SF293.T5O27 2009
636.1'32 — dc22   2008026827

Note to Parents and Teachers

The Horses set supports national science standards related to life science. This book describes and illustrates Thoroughbred horses. The images support early readers in understanding the text. The repetition of words and phrases helps early readers learn new words. This book also introduces early readers to subject-specific vocabulary words, which are defined in the Glossary section. Early readers may need assistance to read some words and to use the Table of Contents, Glossary, Read More, Internet Sites, and Index sections of the book.

Table of Contents

4

A Fast Horse

The Thoroughbred is
a brave horse breed.
These fast horses don't
give up in a race.

Most owners raise
Thoroughbreds to race.
These horses can reach
a top speed of 45 miles
(72 kilometers) per hour.

withers

8

A Thoroughbred's body
is made for running.
It has long legs
and strong hindquarters.
It stands 15 to 17 hands tall.

Horses are measured in hands.
Each hand is 4 inches (10 centimeters).
A horse is measured from the ground
to its withers.

From Foal to Adult

Most Thoroughbred foals
are born in spring.
They begin training
as racehorses
after about 18 months.

Owners enter 2-year-old Thoroughbreds in races. The horses usually race until they are 4 years old. Some race until they are 10.

14

Not Just a Racer

Thoroughbreds have uses other than racing. People ride Thoroughbreds in the sport of polo.

Thoroughbreds take part in horse shows. Dressage shows off the skills of both a horse and its rider.

Thoroughbreds are
great to ride for fun.
Owners ride them on trails
in all kinds of weather.

Thoroughbreds are
born to run.
But thoroughbreds are also
at home in a quiet pasture.

Glossary

brave — fearless

breed — a certain kind of animal within an animal group

dressage — the art of guiding a horse through different movements

foal — a young horse or pony

hindquarter — the part of a horse where the back leg and rump connect to the body

pasture — a grassy area of land where animals can move about freely

polo — a game played on horseback using wooden balls and sticks called mallets

Read More

Green, Emily K. *Horses*. Farm Animals. Minneapolis: Bellwether Media, 2007.

Stone, Lynn M. *Thoroughbred Horses*. Eye to Eye with Horses. Vero Beach, Fla.: Rourke, 2008.

Internet Sites

FactHound offers a safe, fun way to find educator-approved Internet sites related to this book.

Here's what you do:

1. Visit *www.facthound.com*
2. Choose your grade level.
3. Begin your search.

This book's ID number is 9781429622363.

FactHound will fetch the best sites for you!

Index

Word Count: 159
Grade: 1
Early-Intervention Level: 16

Editorial Credits
Erika L. Shores, editor; Bobbi J. Wyss, designer;
    Sarah L. Schuette, photo shoot direction

Photo Credits
Capstone Press/TJ Thoraldson Digital Photography, cover, 1, 6, 8, 10, 12, 20
Shutterstock/Kanwarjit Singh Boparai, 4; Kondrashov Mikhail Evgenevich, 18;
    Margo Harrison, 16; MAT, 14

The Capstone Press Photo Studio thanks Wood-Mere Farms and Canterbury
Downs for their help with photo shoots.

Capstone Press thanks Robert Coleman, PhD, associate professor of
Equine Extension at the University of Kentucky, Lexington's Department
of Animal Sciences, for reviewing this book.